VENICE
THE CITY AT A GLANCE

C000202144

Chiesa del Redentore
Andrea Palladio's church comes to l
during the Festa del Redentore in Jul
a wooden bridge is built across the c
Fondamenta San Giacomo

Chiesa di San Giorgio dei Greci
The Greek community was an important
presence in Renaissance Venice and this
Orthodox church, with its leaning belltower,
was founded in the mid-16th century.
Campo San Zaccaria

Basilica di Santa Maria della Salute
Baldassare Longhena's stunning basilica was
built in thanks after the city survived the 1630
plague, which killed one in three residents.
Campo della Salute

Palazzo Ducale
The residence of the Doge, and home to the
city's council, law courts and prison, is a mix
of Gothic exteriors and classical interiors.
Piazzetta San Marco

Campanile di San Marco
One of the city's most iconic edifices, the
San Marco belltower is the highest structure
in the city at 99m. It was rebuilt in 1912.
Piazza San Marco

Basilica di San Marco
Venice's intoxicating cathedral is a unique
and exotic monument with a world-famous
façade, domes and mosaics.
Piazza San Marco

Molino Stucky
This striking neo-Gothic former flour mill had
1,500 employees in its heyday. It recently
reopened as a hotel after 52 years of closure.
See p016

INTRODUCTION
THE CHANGING FACE OF THE URBAN SCENE

Venice is, of course, eternally beguiling and unique. However, it also has a dwindling, ageing population and is notoriously resistant to change. After La Fenice opera house (Campo San Fantin 1965, T 041 786 511) burned down for the third time in 1996, it was rebuilt to look exactly the same, which many see as symptomatic of the city's inherent provincialism. Yet the new millennium did bring stirrings of change. Sleek eateries and bars have opened, along with hotels, such as Ca Maria Adele (see p017), which merge of-the-moment design with 18th-century-style opulence, or eschew brocade and chandeliers altogether, as at Charming House DD724 (see p030).

Architecturally, things are also moving, if a little lethargically. Modern art spaces have received particular attention. Mario Botta revamped the Fondazione Querini Stampalia gallery (see p064) in 2003, a palazzo already given an overhaul by Carlo Scarpa in the 1950s, and 2006 saw Tadao Ando's renovation of the Palazzo Grassi (see p036). Ando is also sprucing up Renaissance customs house Dogana di Mare (Fondamenta Dogana alla Salute), due to open in 2009 as a museum housing François Pinault's enviable art collection (see p036). Venice's fourth bridge, designed by Santiago Calatrava, was finished in 2007, and David Chipperfield's extension of the Isola di San Michele cemetery is underway, though, as critics point out, it is not destined for the living. Yet it seems La Serenissima is finally starting to wake up to the beauty of modern architecture.

ESSENTIAL INFO

FACTS, FIGURES AND USEFUL ADDRESSES

TOURIST OFFICE
APT Venezia
San Marco 71f
Piazza San Marco
T 041 2424
www.turismovenezia.it

TRANSPORT
Airport Waterboat Service
Alilaguna
T 041 240 1701
www.alilaguna.it
Vaporetti (water buses)
T 041 2424
www.actv.it
Water taxis (24-hour)
Consorzia Motoscafi Venezia
T 041 522 2303
www.motoscafivenezia.it

EMERGENCY SERVICES
Ambulance
T 118
Fire
T 115
Police
T 113
24-hour pharmacy
Check the rota that is displayed in all
pharmacy windows

CONSULATES
British Consulate
Piazzale Donatori di Sangue 2
Mestre
T 041 505 5990
www.ukve.it
US Consulate
Via Principe Amedeo 2-10
Milan
T 02 290 351
www.usembassy.it

MONEY
American Express
Salizzada San Moisè 1471
T 041 520 0844

POSTAL SERVICES
Post Office
Salizzada del Fondaco dei Tedeschi 5554
T 803 160
Shipping
SDA Express Courier
T 199 113 366
www.sda.it

BOOKS
Death in Venice by Thomas Mann (Vintage)
Venice Revealed: An Intimate Portrait
by Paolo Barbaro (Souvenir Press)
Venice: The City and Its Architecture by
Richard Goy and JG Links (Phaidon Press)

WEBSITES
Architecture/Design
www.archinform.net
Art
www.guggenheim-venice.com
www.palazzograssi.it
Newspaper
www.gazzettino.it

COST OF LIVING
**Taxi from Marco Polo Airport
to city centre**
£67.50
Cappuccino
£0.85
Packet of cigarettes
£3.10
Daily newspaper
£0.75
Bottle of champagne
£52.50

VENICE
Area
300 sq km
Population
62,000
Currency: euro
€1 = £0.77 = \$1.55
Telephone codes
Italy: 39
Venice: 041
Time
GMT +1

Budapest ○
Milan ○   □ Venice
Marseille ○
○ Barcelona   ITALY
○ Valencia   Rome ○

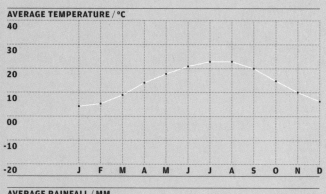

AVERAGE TEMPERATURE / °C

40
30
20
10
00
-10
-20

J F M A M J J A S O N D

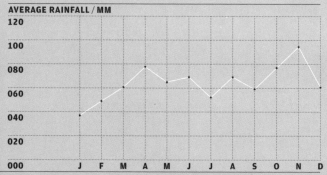

AVERAGE RAINFALL / MM

120
100
080
060
040
020
000

J F M A M J J A S O N D

NEIGHBOURHOODS
THE AREAS YOU NEED TO KNOW AND WHY

To help you navigate the city, we've chosen the most interesting districts (see below and the map inside the back cover) and colour-coded our featured venues, according to their location; those venues that are outside these areas are not coloured.

CANNAREGIO

One of the city's six *sestieri* (districts), this area runs from the low-slung train station (see p066) almost to the Ponte di Rialto (see p034). Though it contains the tacky Strada Nuova, much of the area is quiet and pleasantly ruminative. The old Jewish ghetto is here, as is the Fondamenta Nuove, from where you can take a boat to the pretty Isola di San Michele cemetery and the islands of Murano and Burano beyond.

LA GIUDECCA

Lying just south of Venice proper, this long, thin island has a different feel from the rest of Venice. Historically one of the city's poorest areas, it has undergone much gentrification. The transformation of the 19th-century flour mill at its western end into the large Molino Stucky Hilton hotel (see p016) has helped. La Giudecca is also home to the grande dame of luxury Venetian hotels, the sybaritic and utterly wonderful Cipriani (see p016).

SANTA CROCE AND SAN POLO

This is where you'll find the Rialto market (see p034), with the area around Campo Cesare Battisti having become the city's nightlife and party hub. The hip bars and restaurants here, many with to-die-for views of the Grand Canal, stay open until late. You should also visit Santa Maria Gloriosa dei Frari (see p070), to see some of Venice's most significant art treasures, including two Titian masterpieces.

CASTELLO

The largest *sestiere* in Venice, Castello is dominated by the Arsenale (see p014), formerly a military and shipbuilding powerhouse and largely derelict, although now partly used by the Biennales, the city council or private companies. The Art Biennale's main venue (Giardini della Biennale, T 041 521 8711) is just east of the Arsenale in public gardens inaugurated in 1895 and housing 30 national pavilions.

DORSODURO

This southern district stretches from the docks and working-class Santa Marta to the well-heeled streets around the Salute church (Campo della Salute 1, T 041 274 3911) and old customs house (Fondamenta Dogana alla Salute) in the east. Here you will find Renaissance and modern art in Gallerie dell'Accademia (see p032) and the Peggy Guggenheim Collection (see p032) respectively. Campo Santa Margherita buzzes from dawn until the wee hours.

SAN MARCO

The heart of the city, San Marco has the highest density of attractions, mostly packed into the great square and church that give the *sestiere* its name. Reserve several hours to check out the key sights, and the sweeping view of the city from the Campanile (see p032). Also, make sure you find time to visit the city's most glamorous temporary art space, the Palazzo Grassi (see p036), revamped by Tadao Ando.

LANDMARKS
THE SHAPE OF THE CITY SKYLINE

Even if you've never been to Venice, you will have seen the multiple domes of the Basilica di San Marco (Piazza San Marco) and the intricate stonework of the Ponte di Rialto (see p034) in scores of films and paintings. Such iconic renditions – for example Thomas Mann's multi-layered *Death in Venice* and Nicolas Roeg's haunting *Don't Look Now* – perfectly capture the beauty and intoxicating aura of this magical city built on water. Wandering around its labyrinth of narrow *calle* (alleys), you could easily be transported into a bygone era. But then the dream is broken as you inevitably wind up in the maelstrom of tourists in Rialto, Piazza San Marco and the main thoroughfares connecting them to the station.

Today the city seems to exist on two parallel planes – the one inhabited by the 60,000 remaining Venetians and the one visited by an endless stream of tourists. Don't let that put you off, though. Instead, get around the city the way the locals do – on foot and by *traghetto* (ferry) across the Grand Canal at strategic points – and avoid San Marco during the day and the crowded *vaporetti* if possible. Above all, delve into the heart of each of the six *sestieri*, in particular the less obvious Castello district in the east and Santa Croce in the centre, and you'll probably emerge in a *campo* (square) teeming with children playing, adults gossiping and an almighty Romanesque church. That is the real magic of Venice.
For full addresses, see Resources.

Fondaco dei Turchi

Built in 1225 by an exile from Pesaro, this palace was considered so beautiful that in 1381 it was bought by the republic and used for visiting dignitaries. In 1621 it was leased to Turkish merchants, who used it as a warehouse and residence, even installing a mosque (most likely the first one in Western Europe) and a hammam. After falling into a dismal state of disrepair, it suffered an unhistorical restoration in the 19th century and was almost entirely reconstructed. Its striking pink-and-white marble façade was partly preserved, and its water-level arcade, first-floor loggia and distinctive round arches remain an awe-inspiring example of the Venetian Byzantine style. The building now contains the city's Museum of Natural History. *Salizzada del Fondaco dei Turchi 1730, T 041 275 0206, www.msn.ve.it*

Torre dell'Orologio

The Piazza San Marco is not only home to the Basilica, the Palazzo Ducale and the Campanile (see p032) – take time to admire the iconic clock tower as well. An incredible feat of mechanical precision, it indicates the phase of the moon and the reigning sign of the Zodiac as well as the time. In the past it allowed seafarers to discern the most favourable hour to set out to sea. The tower was commissioned by Doge Agostino Barbarigo in 1493 and constructed by Giampaolo and Giancarlo Rainieri. In 1858, the clock was declared the official timekeeper of Venice, according to which all other devices were set. Swiss watchmaker Piaget spent almost 10 years restoring the clock; it was unveiled in 2006. *Piazza San Marco*

Ca' d'Oro

One of Venice's most famous palazzi, the 15th-century Ca' d'Oro is where the family of Desdemona lives in Orson Welles' film version of *Othello*. This late Gothic palace was given the name Ca' d'Oro – House of Gold – in celebration of its opulent façade, covered in gilded carvings, ultramarine paint and varnished vermilion marble. The ornate decorations have faded, but the façade has survived essentially unscathed, its striking marble columns supporting exotic oriental arches. The interior has been modified by various owners and today houses the Giorgio Franchetti collection, which is dedicated to Venetian, Tuscan and Flemish painting, sculpture and tapestries. The most renowned piece in the gallery is undoubtedly Mantegna's *Saint Sebastian*. *Calle Ca' d'Oro 3932, T 041 520 0345, www.cadoro.org*

Arsenale

This imposing military complex is fronted by an elaborately decorated Renaissance gateway that is guarded by stone lions and various classical statues. Once the largest shipyard in the world, it was begun in 1104 and continually extended from the 14th to the 16th century. During its busiest period, in the 16th century, its 16,000 *Arsenalotti* could build a warship in just 12 hours; for a vivid description of the slaving workers, read Canto XXI of the *Inferno* by Dante, who was inspired by his visits to the shipyard. Although part of the Arsenale is still used by the Italian military, shipbuilding was transferred to private yards more than a century ago. The rest of the building is being restored to provide exhibition and office space. If you visit during one of the Biennales, you can get a glimpse inside.
Rio dell'Arsenale

HOTELS

WHERE TO STAY AND WHICH ROOMS TO BOOK

Venice is not known for sleek, contemporary lodgings. Most of its hotels favour 18th-century Venetian décor: damask, Murano-glass chandeliers, gilt and traditional Venetian flooring. High-luxe veterans such as the Hotel Cipriani (Fondamenta San Giovanni 10, T 041 520 7744) continue to entice visitors, but the noughties have brought a wave of stylish sleepovers, starting with the Ca' Pisani (see p026), followed by the charming Novecento Boutique Hotel (Calle del Dose 2683, T 041 241 3765), minimalist Charming House DD724 (see p030) and lavish Ca Maria Adele (opposite). Recent openings, such as the Palazzo Barbarigo sul Canal Grande (Calle Corner 2765, T 041 740 172), are maintaining the momentum.

A couple of traditional luxury options arrived in 2007 – the fairly distinctive Molino Stucky Hilton (Fondamenta San Biagio 810, T 041 272 3311), set in a neo-Gothic former flour mill, and the Ca' Sagredo (see p019). Two further major projects are slated for 2008: Palazzina Grassi (Calle Grassi 3247, T 041 528 4644), in a 1500s building with up-to-date interpretations of traditional décor, and the tentatively named Centurion, set to lure hip travellers to the most atmospheric part of Dorsoduro. The restaurant-cum-hotel trend has also hit town. The eaterie Avogaria (see p059) opened three elegant rooms in autumn 2007, and neo-baroque nightclub 947 Club (www.947club.com) is due to open four rooms in 2008. *For full addresses and room rates, see Resources.*

Ca Maria Adele

Currently the most romantic hotel in Venice, the Ca Maria Adele opened in early 2004. It has built up a loyal and occasionally celebrity-studded clientele but it refuses to rest on its laurels, adding communal areas and a new suite (with a chromotherapy jacuzzi at the foot of the super-king bed) and changing the décor. Choose between the minimalist glamour of the nine deluxe rooms, such as 119 (above), and suites (339 boasts a sumptuous terrace) or reserve one of the five 'concept' rooms. For instance, La Sala Noir is a sensual blend of chocolate and aubergine with a black chandelier. A Moroccan-inspired terrace under the dome of the Basilica di Santa Maria della Salute is a great spot for breakfast.
Rio Terà dei Catecumeni 111,
T 041 520 3078, www.camariaadele.it

Ca' Gottardi

Just off the Strada Nuova, in an area where there is a dearth of alluring hotels and eateries, this boutique pad neatly fills a void. Its all-white stark staircase, Zen pool and other designer touches are slightly at odds with the conventional yet comfortable rooms. The nicest accommodation can be found in the *dépendance* that's just steps away; Room 36 is a corner bedroom with several windows, suffused light and a sexy vibe, while Suite 28 (above) is the luxe option. Work by local artists is regularly exhibited in the main hall and lounge, there's a breakfast room only feet away from the water and there are plans to renovate another floor of the *dépendance*. *Strada Nuova 2283, T 041 275 9333, www.cagottardi.com*

Ca' Sagredo

This 15th-century palazzo is not just a hotel but also a national monument. As you climb the sweeping main staircase (above), flanked by marble cherubs and leading through to the music room, admire the frescoes by Pietro Longhi and Giambattista Tiepolo and take on board the uniqueness of this accommodation. Its original owner, Count Sagredo, was a man who was equally taken by pleasures of the flesh and the intellect, it seems. Both his library and bedroom, complete with secret stairwell for his mistresses, have been transformed into Room 103 and Grand Canal Suite Prestige (overleaf) respectively, which are grand, historic and intimate all at the same time. The L'Alcova restaurant attracts in-the-know Venetians. *Campo Santa Sofia 4198, T 041 241 3111, www.casagredohotel.com*

Grand Canal Suite Prestige, Ca' Sagredo

Casa de Uscoli

Though the dilapidated entrance is less than promising, Casa de Uscoli is actually a bit of a find. Just off the Campo Santo Stefano, overlooking the Gallerie dell' Accademia (T 041 520 0345) on the Grand Canal, it's a Renaissance palazzo with three rooms and three apartments quirkily decked out by charismatic Spanish owner Alejandro Suárez Díaz de Bethencourt. He has adorned the place with works by Fontana, Castiglioni and Matthias Schaller, books packed into shelves all around, and overhead lamps (right), which he designed himself. The furnishings are elegant, if a little scuffed, and home-baked goodies are served at breakfast in a piano room (right). Opt for the cute Suite dell'Alcova (above) or the Suite della Salute with its superb views; all at a fraction of the price of a luxury hotel.
Campo Santo Stefano 2818,
T 041 241 0669, www.casadeuscoli.com

Hotel Metropole

This four-star with an enviable location has been a hotel since 1880 and in the hands of the Beggiato family since 1970. It is famous for its luxurious décor; the owners' extraordinary collections of antique purses, visiting-card holders, trunks, crucifixes, bottle openers and nutcrackers; and jovial staff who have worked there for decades. Now daughter Gloria has taken over the day-to-day running of the hotel and updated many of the rooms and lounge areas. Bedrooms range from quirky and cool – Room 405 (left) has 1940s furniture and an art deco vibe – to traditional and opulent – the top-floor Damasco Suite offers views of the Bacino di San Marco and a mother-of-pearl fountain pool in the lounge. Met, its Michelin-starred restaurant, is another reason to love the Hotel Metropole.
Riva degli Schiavoni 4149, T 041 520 5044, www.hotelmetropole.com

Ca' Pisani

Venice's original designer hotel was opened in 2000 by the Serandrei family, who have owned the Hotel Saturnia (T 041 520 8377) on Calle Larga XXII Marzo since the early 20th century. This beautiful late-14th-century merchant townhouse is filled with 1930s and 1940s furniture and art-deco design inspired by the futurist artists of the 1920s. The main hues on display are mustard yellow, orange, beige and grey; the bathrooms have deep hydro-massage baths; and each bedroom — such as a Standard Room (above) — features a 1940s bed, intricate woodwork, leather armchairs and silver-leaf wardrobes and desks. Choose a Junior Suite (right) for even more luxury. The top floor has three rooms with stunning views, a Turkish bath and a rooftop terrace with sunbeds, and a shower for cooling off between cocktails. *Rio Terà António Foscarini 979a, T 041 240 1411, www.capisanihotel.it*

Ca' Nigra Lagoon Resort
Located in one of the oldest buildings
in Venice (a 13th-century former wool
workshop), Ca' Nigra is surrounded by
a large garden overlooking the Canal
Grande. It is comfortable and very quiet,
and Room 11 (pictured) stands out for
its glass-encased bathroom and a round
bed that still manages to be tasteful.
Campo San Simeon Grande 927,
T 041 275 0047, www.hotelcanigra.com

Charming House DD724

The DD724 is more of a sleek B&B than
a hotel. Its six rooms, such as the Superior
Room (left), feature abstract art, neutral
tones and occasional lashings of colour
in the form of a throw, a Moroso armchair
or pillows. In late 2006, Charming House
DD694 opened down the road with a suite
that can accommodate a family, and in
autumn 2007 the same team inaugurated
IQs (T 041 241 0062), a hip condo hotel off
Campo Santa Maria Formosa. In the words
of owner Chiara Bocchini, who created the
interiors of all three venues with architect/
photographer Mauro Mazzolini, at IQs you
can expect the service of a hotel but the
feel of a home. Its four apartments adhere
to mostly dark colour themes and look
on to water, while the reception area is
in a former *cavana* (where gondolas are
parked) and bathed in watery light.
*Ramo da Mula 724, T 041 277 0262,
www.dd724.it*

24 HOURS
SEE THE BEST OF THE CITY IN JUST ONE DAY

With its numerous bridges, steps and maze of alleys, wandering around Venice is a workout for both your calves and your brain. However, the city centre is compact, so you're never far from a landmark. Start off early in the morning to avoid the crowds at Piazza San Marco and its many sights – the opulent Basilica di San Marco, the views from the top of the Campanile, the pink-and-white Palazzo Ducale and its Bridge of Sighs.

After an obligatory coffee (opposite), head to Rialto market (see p034) for some local fare and atmosphere. Renaissance fans should visit the Gallerie dell'Accademia (Campo della Carità 1050, T 041 522 2247) or any of the myriad churches. If contemporary culture is more your thing, drop in to the Peggy Guggenheim Collection (Calle San Cristoforo 704, T 041 240 5411) or Palazzo Grassi (see p036), which was cleverly restored by Tadao Ando in 2006. Even if you're not in town for the city's famous art, architecture and film festivals, the Biennale foundation (www.labiennale.org) puts on exhibitions and concerts in unique venues throughout the year.

The city's restaurant scene is leaving its mediocre past behind. Riviera (see p038) serves seafood in elegant surrounds; for more innovative cuisine, head to Naranzaria (see p048). After dinner, sip a cocktail in Aurora (see p055) or Harry's Bar (see p039), then make your way to late-night hot spot Centrale (see p056).
For full addresses, see Resources.

10.30 Torrefazione Marchi

You'll know you're close to this popular bar before you even see it, as the heady smell of coffee pervades the surrounding neighbourhood. This roaster (one of just two left in town, and the only one that sells to the public) opened in 1930 and has changed very little over the decades. The focus is on coffee, coffee and more coffee, a lot of it packed in jute bags piled high on the shop floor. And you know it's good because you'll be sharing standing room with huddles of local workers stopping by for a caffeine fix or housewives meeting for a gossip. Try the *caffè della sposa* (made from eight of the best Arabica blends) or a *Veneziano* (coffee, cocoa and milk foam). *Rio Terà San Leonardo 1337, T 041 716 371*

11.30 Rialto market

At the north-western foot of the Rialto bridge (right), from Monday to Saturday, this buzzy market is bursting with tasty local produce – often signalled by the word *nostrano* (ours) – from the nearby islands of Sant'Erasmo, Mazzorbo and Vignole. Stop for a prosecco at Al Marcà (Campo Cesare Battisti 213), a simple hole in the wall and one of the area's original bars, and sample some tasty *cichetti* (Venetian snacks) from the local institution Do Mori (Calle dei Do Mori 429). Choose from dishes such as marinated artichokes, tuna *polpette* (fishballs), *sarde in saor* (sweet-and-sour sardines and onions), bread topped with cheeses or *baccalà mantecato* (dry cod whipped into a creamy spread). And do like the Venetians do, and wash it all down with an *ombra*, a glass of local red or white wine.
Around Campo Cesare Battisti

14.30 Palazzo Grassi
Giorgio Massari's 18th-century palace
was bought by the French modern
art collector and luxury goods tycoon
François Pinault and sympathetically
restored by the Japanese architect
Tadao Ando in 2006. It now functions
as a stunning marble backdrop for a
revolving programme of art exhibitions.
*Campo San Samuele 3231,
T 041 523 1680, www.palazzograssi.it*

20.00 Riviera

This recently revamped, traditional eaterie is renowned for its excellent seafood and comes highly recommended by discerning Venetians. There's a formal dining room or outdoor seating beside the canal for sunnier days. The homemade pastas are delicious, in particular the lobster *trenette* (ribbon pasta), and radicchio and scampi risotto; for mains, try the lamb chops in a blueberry sauce, or *fritto misto* (delicately fried fish and seafood). Then splurge on a classic Italian pudding, such as panna cotta or tiramisu, and accompany it with a dessert wine from the extensive selection. *Fondamenta Zattere 1473, T 041 522 7621, www.ristoranteriviera.it*

22.30 Harry's Bar

It's said that you haven't been to Venice until you've dropped in to Harry's. It may be cramped and pricey, but this legendary 1930s locale, now run by Arrigo Cipriani, son of founder Giuseppe, is a Venetian institution, with a stylish ambience and classically simple décor. A former haunt of Ernest Hemingway, the venue still pulls in Hollywood stars and tourists alike. Order a Bellini (the peach and prosecco cocktail that made Harry's famous) and then head upstairs to soak up the atmosphere and enjoy the spectacular views over the Grand Canal to the Basilica di Santa Maria della Salute.
Calle Vallaresso 1323, T 041 528 5777, www.cipriani.com

URBAN LIFE

CAFÉS, RESTAURANTS, BARS AND NIGHTCLUBS

Eating out in Venice has, up until recently, been hit and miss, with many restaurants gearing themselves towards an undiscerning tourist crowd, using cheap ingredients to make pedestrian dishes. But the city is finally welcoming a hipper breed of restaurants and bars. The hot new part of town – the area around Rialto market (see p034), specifically Campo dell'Erbaria and Campo Cesare Battisti – is a good place to start (and finish) your investigations.

For a light snack, head to Impronta Café (Crosera San Pantalon 3815, T 041 275 0386), or stop for a coffee at Caffè del Doge (Calle dei Cinque 609, T 041 522 7787). The pizzeria Il Refolo (Campo San Giacomo dell'Orio 1459, T 041 524 0016) boasts a delightful terrace in summer. Foodies in search of a low-key gourmet meal should try Mistrà (Fondamenta San Giacomo 212a, T 041 522 0743), located in a boat-repair yard. Also on Giudecca, La Palanca (Fondamenta del Ponte Piccolo 448, T 041 528 7719) is a panoramic lunch spot. For *aperitivi,* there are superb views from Bancogiro (Campo San Giacometto 122, T 041 523 2061), or try the glam 947 Club (Campo Santissimi Filippo e Giacomo 4337, T 041 528 5686) or the informal Un Mondo Di Vino (Salizzada San Canciano 5984a, T 041 521 1093). After sundown, don your designer jeans and heels and dine out in style at Muro Vino e Cucina (Campo Cesare Battisti già Bella Vienna 222, T 041 523 7495) or Naranzaria (see p048). *For full addresses, see Resources.*

Il Ridotto

This innovative and intimate 12-seat eaterie features exposed brick, mirrors, coloured Murano glasses, Versace coffee cups and Rosenthal plates. Charismatic patron/chef Gianni Bonaccorsi is on hand to guide you through the seasonal menu or suggest the day's specials, which vary according to the fare available at the market. You'll be offered the freshest fish, such as a trio of tartares made with salmon, mullet and red prawns, often served with various tangy fruit and vegetable concoctions, and dishes with imaginative twists, such as black squid ink tortelli (a larger type of tortellini) filled with sea bass. Bonaccorsi is also an Italian wine expert, and the drinks list here is as impressive as the cuisine.
Campo Santi Filippo e Giacomo 4509, T 041 520 8280, www.hoteltiepolo.com

Osteria San Marco

One venue to shake up the often overpriced and mediocre Venetian restaurant scene, especially given its proximity to touristy Piazza San Marco, is Osteria San Marco. Under the dynamic management of Venetians Carlo Siviero, Fabio Rigo, Luca Dei Rossi and Massimo Guadagni, this revamped old-timer now has six-month rotating art exhibitions on exposed brick walls, atmospheric lighting and a glass counter filled with regional cheeses and jams. The focus is on high-quality spirits and wines, with some excellent Veneto labels and more than 30 varieties offered by the glass (bottles and cases of wine adorn every nook and cranny), and equally distinctive food. Your John Dory might come lightly fried in a crunchy sesame seed crust or your scampi served in a light spinach frittata. Homemade desserts and pasta complete a memorable experience.
Frezzeria 1610, T 041 528 5242

Vecio Fritolin

After a period in the doldrums, this old-style Venetian *fritolin* is now going full steam once more in the capable hands of diminutive present owner Irina Freguia. The setting is classical (wooden beams, typical Venetian flooring, red tablecloths and hanging pots and pans), but the short, fish-oriented menu is far more innovative than the surroundings may suggest. The signature dish is a cocoa-infused rice tagliatelle served with *mazzancolle* prawns and courgettes. In a nod to its humble fish-and-chip-shop beginnings, passers-by can purchase a *scartosso de pesce* (a paper cone filled with lightly battered fish) for £6. The same team is behind the café/restaurant in the modern art mecca Palazzo Grassi (see p036). *Calle della Regina 2262, T 041 522 2881, www.veciofritolin.it*

Skyline Bar

The Molino Stucky Hilton (see p016) itself may be humongous, unwieldy and too standard issue for the discerning design-conscious traveller, but its eighth-floor Skyline Bar alone is worth the *vaporetto* ride. Go at sunset and take your cocktails on one of the two terraces – either overlooking Giudecca island and San Marco in the distance; or out over the lagoon towards the smoky skyline of the industrial town of Marghera on the mainland. While you're up here, check out the city's only rooftop pool (see p094).
Molino Stucky Hilton, Fondamenta San Biagio 810, T 041 272 3311, www.molinostuckyhilton.com

Lineadombra

This restaurant has an alluring location with a direct view across the canal to the Zitelle and Redentore churches. While the rest of the city simmers in the summer heat, you'll be assured a breeze on the large floating terrace (above). Inside, the slick, modern interiors, including a first-floor private room with an amazing view, are a rarity. An army of attractive waiters serves up dishes such as *millefoglie* of scampi with onions, raisins and apples; *granseola* crab, raw courgette and lemon cheesecake; sea bass served with capers and vanilla-infused potatoes; or pasta made on the premises, washed down with a tipple from the list of more than 600 wines. Top it off with a slice of banana and strawberry cake or fig and walnut cake. *Ponte dell'Umiltà 19, T 041 241 1881, www.ristorantelineadombra.com*

Naranzaria

In the heart of the Rialto market area (see p034), this wine bar and *osteria* opened to a lot of hype due to its fabulous Grand Canal location and its noble owner, Count Brandino Brandolini d'Adda, whose family makes award-winning wines in the nearby region of Friuli. Mostly it has lived up to the billing, and it is certainly a more sophisticated and better-quality option than its neighbours. A good choice for *aperitivi* and cocktails, it also offers a fusion menu of sushi, including a tuna, mozzarella and tomato variety, created by Brazilian/Japanese chef Akira, flavourful cold cuts from Friuli, various carpaccios and couscous with prawns.
Campo dell'Erbaria 130, T 041 724 1035, www.naranzaria.it

Andrea Zanin
From a distance it looks like a jewellery
store, but this minimalist, Piero Lissoni-
designed space is actually a pâtisserie,
selling exquisite fruit and chocolate
mousses, pralines and elaborate bite-
sized cakes and tarts made by award-
winning local pastry chef Andrea Zanin.
Eat standing up with an espresso at the
7m-long stone-and-glass counter.
Campo San Luca 4589, T 041 522 4803

Restaurant De Pisis and B-Bar

Situated in one of the most enchanting spots in Venice – where the Grand Canal meets the Bacino di San Marco – with the sounds of moored gondolas bumping prows in the background, De Pisis is run by acclaimed young chef Giovanni Ciresa, who made his name at Tuscany's two-Michelin-starred Enoteca Pinchiorri, and alternates between Mediterranean and Asian cuisines with considerable finesse. Sample dishes include turbot in chestnut leaves, and porcini and ginger risotto. After your meal head to the iconic B-Bar (in the same hotel), a cult nightspot in the 1970s and back in favour with Venice's cool set. The 1950s vibe is achieved courtesy of gold walls, marble floors, lounge chairs and a grand piano, and the sound system for DJ sets upstairs is a cut above.
Bauer Hotel, Campo San Moisè 1459,
T 041 520 7022, www.bauervenezia.com

Osteria Santa Marina

Deservedly renowned for its elaborate cuisine and simple but effective twists on traditional Venetian dishes, Osteria Santa Marina is elegant and upmarket, with a beamed ceiling, glass-fronted cabinets, a polished dark-wood bar, hanging metal lampshades and windows overlooking a tranquil *campo*. Culinary delights include black barley risotto with puréed pumpkin and grilled shrimp; tiny grilled *calamaretti* served on a bed of lime-fragranced potatoes; and baked pilgrim scallops with a purée of green peas and basil oil. If you still have room, finish with a lemon sorbet with liquorice, or apple cake and cinnamon ice cream, and then coffee served with tiny and delicious homemade biscuits. Service is attentive, and the sommelier is a mine of information.

Campo Santa Marina 5911, T 041 528 5239

Aurora

This is a good example of how younger Venetians are attempting to reclaim their city, especially the extremely touristy San Marco area. Located in the ultimate Venice square – Piazza San Marco – Aurora is where thirtysomethings congregate well beyond the curfew of its stuffier, overpriced piazza counterparts Ristorante Gran Caffè Quadri (T 041 522 2105) and Caffè Florian (T 041 520 5641), for its happening DJ sets and live gigs. In summer, a sister venue opens on Lido island (see p090), called Aurora Beach (T 041 526 8013).
Piazza San Marco 48-50, T 041 528 6405, www.aurora.st

Centrale Restaurant Lounge
This glamorous warehouse-style venue wouldn't be out of place in New York, but in Venice it's a one-off. You can eat and drink until past 2am – order a Rossini (prosecco and fresh strawberries) and sink into a divan. If you arrive by boat, one entrance opens directly onto a canal. You don't get more Venetian than that.
Piscina Frezzeria 1659b, T 041 296 0664, www.centrale-lounge.com

Avogaria

Opened in 2002, Avogaria was just about the first venue in the city to adopt a stylish minimalist design. Architect and owner Francesco Pugliese has created an elegant combination of poured concrete flooring, the odd iridescent blue wall, exposed brickwork, hanging shelves, frosted-glass portholes and brushed-steel-and-wood tables. The space has proved a hit with locals, who appreciate the clean interiors and delicious authentic Puglian cooking of chef Antonella (Francesco's sister), such as *fusilli salentini* with artichokes and shrimps and *orecchiette* with meat in tomato sauce. Her husband Mimmo Piccolomo serves clients with exceptional bonhomie. The trio recently opened three guest rooms (see p016) next door, two of which have their own enchanting garden.
Calle dell'Avogaria 1629, T 041 296 0491, www.avogaria.com

Dogado Lounge
This bar offers fusion dining, fantastic cocktails, DJ sets and jazz concerts in a part of town lacking in decent nocturnal venues. The major selling point is the massive, partly canopied terrace, and inside, the theatrically lit 18th-century palazzo is filled with Murano chandeliers and pearl Murano curtains. Intimate corners and low-slung divans abound.
Strada Nuova 3662, T 041 520 8544

INSIDER'S GUIDE

ISOTTA DARDILLI, CREATIVE DIRECTOR

Lifelong Venice resident Isotta Dardilli works in Treviso as creative director for Fabrica (www.fabrica.it), Benetton's communications and research centre. She starts her day in Venice with an espresso at Caffè Rosso (Campo Santa Margherita 2963, T 041 528 7998), before heading to Pasticceria Rizzardini (Campo San Polo 1415, T 041 522 3835) to sample the best *krapfen* (doughnuts) in town. Her top lunch spot is Bancogiro (see p040) for its canalside seats and creative, pasta-free menu. If she has friends in town, she takes them to see Tintoretto's paintings at the Scuola Grande di San Rocco (Campo San Rocco 3052, T 041 523 4864), and the nearby Santa Maria Gloriosa dei Frari (see p068). She then introduces them to the best ice cream in Venice at Alaska (Calle Larga dei Bari 1159, T 041 715 211), where Carlo Pistacchi specialises in unusual, additive-free flavours, such as green tea, wasabi and cardamom.

For an *aperitivo*, she heads to Osteria Alla Botte (Calle della Bissa 5482, T 041 520 9775) or Al Marcà (Campo Cesare Battisti 213); the latter is by the Rialto bridge – the city's nocturnal hub, where bars and eateries throb until the early hours. For dinner, Dardilli books a table at the ultra-Venetian and very picturesque Alla Vedova (Ramo del Ca' d'Oro 3912, T 041 528 5324). Afterwards, it's on to Bauer Hotel's glamorous B-Bar (see p052) for celebrity-spotting and the best cocktails and live music in the city.
For full addresses, see Resources.

ARCHITOUR
A GUIDE TO VENICE'S ICONIC BUILDINGS

There's no doubt that Venice has been adept at preserving and celebrating its dense and amazing Byzantine, Gothic, Renaissance and baroque heritage. Yet it also has some rather less beautiful 19th-century districts that could benefit from renovation. In the 20th century, however, there have been some architectural gems. Casa Gardella alle Zattere (opposite) is a minor masterpiece; while Carlo Scarpa's interior for the former Olivetti Showroom (Piazza San Marco) and his renovation of the 16th-century Fondazione Querini Stampalia gallery (Santa Maria Formosa 5252, T 041 271 1411) in the late 1950s and early 1960s were celebrated as examples of his mastery of different materials. However, Pier Luigi Nervi and Angelo Scattolin's 1963 Cassa di Risparmio building (Campo Manin) is considered anodyne rather than forward-looking.

Projects that have been green-lighted sometimes wait decades to come to fruition, or are subsequently rejected. Two schemes that are stuck in drawing-board limbo are the Miralle/Tagliabue-EMBT building for the IUAV (Venice University Institute of Architecture) and Frank Gehry's typically curvaceous Gateway hotel, conference centre and dock near Venice airport. On a brighter note, Santiago Calatrava's fourth bridge over the Grand Canal – erected in 2007 and linking the train station to the Piazzale Roma car park and bus terminal – represents the dawn of a new architectural era. *For full addresses, see Resources.*

Casa Gardella alle Zattere

This superb L-shaped building by Ignazio Gardella was built between 1953 and 1958 and is a modern version of a typical medieval Venetian courtyard house. The entrance connects to two separate groups of flats, one facing out to La Giudecca and the other opening onto an interior garden. Both blocks are six storeys high and made with traditional materials, such as the local travertine used for the bases and trims. The window frames, balustrades, chimneys and doorways feature subtle references to 13th-century architectural ideas. Gardella was a great exponent of Italian rationalism, although he refused to be restricted by its limitations, and this building proved that modern architecture could be highly sensitive to its setting.
Fondamenta delle Zattere 401/
Calle dello Zucchero

Stazione Ferroviaria Santa Lucia

Venice's low-slung railway station is the gateway to the city. Some 82,000 people pass through daily (30 million a year) and for many this is one of the few modern buildings they'll see during their stay. The station was the work of three architects over almost three decades. Chief engineer for the state railways company, Ferrovie dello Stato (FS), Angiolo Mazzoni worked on various designs in the 1920s before a competition awarded construction to the collaborative efforts of Mazzoni and Venetian Virgilio Vallot. Building began in 1936 and continued until 1943 but the station gained its current appearance only in 1950 when FS in-house engineer Paolo Perilli completed the job. The structure is earmarked for further change as part of Italy's ambitious Grandi Stazioni project.
Fondamenta Santa Lucia

Ex-Saffa housing development
On the site of the former industrial area
Saffa, these *case popolari* (social housing
for low-income residents and the elderly)
were designed by the Venetian stiudio
Gregotti Associati and construction began
in 1981. Arranged around ersatz courtyards,
this complex featuring six low apartment
blocks is crisscrossed by different-sized
paths (many lined with trees) that lead
in and around the flats. Though the feeling
is somewhat akin to wandering around
a Club Med village, the homes do show
thoughtful touches designed to make
them blend in with the rest of the urban
fabric. They have been painted an ochre
that matches the bricks of neighbouring
houses and are lined with balconies similar
to the *altane* decorating old palazzi.
*East of Canale di Cannaregio, between
Rio di San Giobbe and Rio della Crea*

Santa Maria Gloriosa dei Frari
Known as i Frari, this immense 13th- to
14th-century Gothic church was built by
the Franciscans and is the tallest church
in Venice after the Basilica di San Marco.
The Franciscans believed in asceticism
so i Frari is fittingly austere, yet it houses
some amazing art, including two Titian
masterpieces: his *Assumption of the Virgin*
over the altar, which exhibits a Venetian
love of colour and texture; and the *Pesaro
Madonna*, unusually showing the Virgin
on the right-hand side of the canvas
instead of in the centre. The church's
other masterwork is Giovanni Bellini's
triptych on wood, the *Madonna and Child*.
Canova's mausoleum (only his heart is
buried within) and Titian's tomb are also
here. Make sure you also visit the Scuola
Grande di San Rocco art gallery (see
p062), with its fantastic cycle of canvases
by Tintoretto, just around the corner.
Campo dei Frari 3072, T 041 275 0462

SHOPPING
THE BEST RETAIL THERAPY AND WHAT TO BUY

There is more to Venice than cheap mass-produced glass clowns and overpriced couture. If you have time and patience, you can find truly original, authentic and tasteful local wares, including traditional crafts that have been produced in the city for centuries. For glassware, take a ferry from Fondamenta Nuove to Murano Collezioni (opposite) on the island of Murano, or head to the most enticing glass shop in town – Massimo Micheluzzi (see p077); for papier-mâché Carnevale masks, the quality is high at Tragicomica (Calle dei Nomboli 2800, T 041 721 102); other Venice essentials include lush brocades, damasks and velvets, and paper.

   Lace was once a staple trade on the island of Burano but it is now mostly imported, though you can still find some authentic pieces along Calle de la Canonica. Another Venice-only shopping experience is to be had at Ghezzo-Segalin (Calle dei Fuseri 4365, T 041 522 2115), where 18th-century replica shoes are made to measure by Daniela Ghezzo, the pupil of now retired shoe-meister Rolando Segalin. And if you want to go down the high-fashion route, the major designer labels are located around San Marco, especially on Calle Larga XXII Marzo, Salizzada San Moisè and Calle Vallaresso. While you're in the area, check out the recently opened Bottega Veneta (Campo San Moisè 1461, T 041 520 6197), the local luxury leather brand's second store in the city.
For full addresses, see Resources.

Murano Collezioni

The city's glassworks moved to Murano from Venice in the 13th century because they were a fire hazard. Many of those still in business now line the Fondamenta dei Vetrai, the canal-side walkway leading away from the island's main landing stage that is populated by many eye-bruisingly touristy and tacky stores. There are a few gems along the way, however. One of these is this warehouse-type Venini and Carlo Moretti outlet with museum-like displays of glass lit by large metallic bell-shaped lamps. The wares range from priceless antiques by designer/architects such as Carlo Scarpa and Gio Ponti to pieces by the doyen of modernist Venetian glass artists himself, Moretti, including this 'Olla' vase (above), £165.
Fondamenta Manin 1c-d, Murano,
T 041 736 272, www.muranocollezioni.com

Angela Greco

Buy beautiful handmade lampshades covered with genuine Fortuny fabric at this jam-packed boutique. The ever-smiling, sixtysomething, pinafore-wearing Greco sisters, Rosy and Rita, have run this shop for 47 years. They make their custom-made lampshades, many of them plissé, out back, and have been popular with wealthy Venetians for decades, decking out luxury hotels both in town and abroad. Coming to Angela Greco is like taking a journey back in time, especially once you get the sisters started on past and present life in Venice (Rosy is the voluble one). If you want to know what the likes of Peggy Guggenheim got up to, they can tell you. *Ponte delle Ostreghe 2433, T 041 523 4573*

Antonia Miletto

This small, sparse, orange-themed shop is filled with subtle jewellery designed by Antonia Miletto and made by skilled artisans in Milan and Florence. Miletto studied gems and architecture, and this is reflected in her jewellery designs. Her pieces are sold in New York, but this is her first and only store, showcasing her unique range of spiralling gold bracelets and diamond-studded ebony rings. Many of her designs combine exotic woods (macassar, purpleheart, cocobolo and ebony) with semi-precious and precious stones (turquoise, amethyst, diamonds and mother-of-pearl). Miletto was among the first to experiment with the tough plastic methacrylic resin, and her collection includes a number of these pieces.
Salizzada Malipiero 3208a,
T 041 520 5177, www.antoniamiletto.com

Massimo Micheluzzi

This gallery/studio near the Gallerie dell' Accademia (T 041 520 0345) is where to come for Murano glassware with a twist. Massimo Micheluzzi took an indirect route to design, studying history of architecture before working in the family antiques business for many years, specialising in glass. It was after getting involved with the production of designs by Laura de Santillana (Paolo Venini's granddaughter) in 1990 that he became enamoured of the creative energy of the Murano furnaces. His personal take on this centuries-old tradition, a highly collectable series of monochromatic vases and vessels, has a strong sculptural quality that shows his fusion of classic Murano techniques (murrine, deep-cutting and cold carving) and a contemporary flair for design. *Calle della Toletta 1071, T 041 528 2190*

VizioVirtù

You could be forgiven for thinking you'd died and gone to chocolate heaven in this temple to all things cocoa. Chocolatier Mariangela Penzo has mastered and updated this centuries-old Venetian tradition, coming up with such quirky delights as ganaches laced with Barolo Chinato wine, tobacco or balsamic vinegar; dragees filled with ginger or coffee beans; and chocolates made with that staple of Venetian cuisine, the pumpkin. There is also a cocoa-rich array of spreads, *semifreddo* desserts and mousses. On a chilly day, pop in for a mug of spicy hot chocolate; in summer, you'll find the iced chocolate drink surprisingly refreshing. If you can't do without your fix once you get home, you can always order online.
Calle del Campaniel 2898a, T 041 275 0149, www.viziovirtu.com

Le Forcole di Saverio Pastor

In this attractively laid-out workshop near
the Basilica di Santa Maria della Salute
(T 041 522 5558), Saverio Pastor hand-
carves oars and *forcole* (oar-rests) for
gondolas and other boats (he is one of
only four remaining craftsmen in Venice,
the only city in the world to vaunt this
profession). *Forcole* are made from walnut
or cherry wood and each takes about 20
hours to complete. More akin to works
of art, with their unusual and complex
lines, there are examples at New York's
Metropolitan Museum of Art and in the
private collections of architects IM Pei
and Frank Gehry. Pastor has been savvy
enough to realise that to stay afloat he
must diversify – hence the scale models
on sale to tourists. Rather than being
tacky though, they are one of Venice's
most beautiful and memorable souvenirs.
*Fondamenta Soranzo 341, T 041 522 5699,
www.forcole.com*

Marina e Susanna Sent

The Sent sisters opened their beautifully stripped-back shop in a piazza near the Peggy Guggenheim Collection (see p032) in 1995. But glass-making has been their Murano-based family's lifeblood for three generations. Their eminently wearable glass jewellery is for sale in various shops and museum stores around the world, but this is where you can buy the entire range, including the remarkable *incamiciato* multilayered vases and delicate glass clutches. Also on sale are exquisite pieces by the talented Venetian glass artist Laura de Santillana and designer Paola Navone. The inspired flat-pack paper packaging alone is worth making a purchase.
Campo San Vio 669, T 041 527 4665

Trois

People often walk past this cramped, old-fashioned store without a moment's thought. Venture inside, however, and you will discover reams of exquisite Fortuny fabrics – Trois has been Venice's exclusive purveyor for the past 50 years. Mariano Fortuny was born in Granada, Spain, in 1871 and studied painting in his homeland, sculpture in Paris, architecture in Rome, and chemistry and dyeing techniques in Germany. In 1920, he invented a method of printing onto fabric that replicated the depth and colour of antique brocades, velvets and tapestries. All the fabrics sold at Trois are based on stunning original designs that are still in production today on the island of Giudecca.
Campo San Maurizio 2666, T 041 522 2905

Attombri

This museum-like space is the stunning
second showcase for jeweller brothers
Stefano and Daniele Attombri – the
original store can be found in Rialto
(T 041 521 2524). They make each of
their elaborate one-of-a-kind jewellery
pieces and objets d'art by hand, often
incorporating antique Murano glass
beads (they bought bags of tiny, historic
conterie beads from a Murano factory
when it closed down) and stunning
beads of their own design. Silvery
nickel-free threads and metals that
change colour with the light beautifully
encapsulate the city's relationship
with the water. Romeo Gigli and Dolce
& Gabbana are fans, and use the brothers'
pieces to accessorise their collections.
*Campo San Maurizio 2668a, T 041 521 0789,
www.attombri.com*

Studio Mirabilia
This veritable treasure trove of weird and wonderful creations is the realm of Gigi Bon, an artist whose bronze rhinoceroses, two-headed lions and surreal paintings pay homage to Venice's sacred symbols. Even if you can't find a home for a rhino with a gondola's comb-shaped *ferro* for horns, you'll be won over by the sheer talent on display.
Calle Malipiero 3084, T 041 523 9570

SPORTS AND SPAS
WORK OUT, CHILL OUT OR JUST WATCH

One could argue that climbing Venice's myriad bridges and steps is sport enough, but the truth is that Venetians can't get enough of outdoor activities, especially if they are connected to the water that surrounds them. Most Venetians own a boat, in which they zip dangerously fast around the lagoon, especially in the summer, when they flock to the beaches of Punto Sabbioni, Jesolo and Lido (see p090); getting *una tintarella* (a tan) is a national obsession.

Even more popular, however, are spectator sports; dozens of waterborne competitions and festivals take place throughout the year. Held on the first Sunday in September, the Regata Storica, a spectacular parade along the Grand Canal, featuring typical 16th-century-style vessels and followed by four races, has been going since the 15th century. Even more impressive is the 30km Vogalonga race (www.vogalonga.it), held in late May and early June. Open to anyone with a craft, it attracts more than 5,000 rowers from Venice, other parts of Italy and around the world.

For those wishing to purify and cleanse in this city of water, La Serenissima offers two alluring pampering palaces. The Palladio Spa (opposite), set in a converted 15th-century convent, has divine products and a minimalist design. Also on Giudecca, the Molino Stucky Hilton hotel boasts a 600 sq m facility with state-of-the-art equipment and a wonderful rooftop pool (see p094).
For full addresses, see Resources.

Palladio Spa

Venice's largest spa may be located a five-minute walk away in the Hilton (see p094) but this one, set in a 15th-century convent-turned-hotel, is the most sophisticated and beautiful. Separated into various spaces, the two that stand out are the gold and green relaxation room (above), with its one-way mirror windows offering views of San Marco, and the opulent jacuzzi room (large mosaic tub, soft-as-butter chaises longues, high, wood-beamed ceilings and a fireplace). The eight beautifully perfumed and lit minimalist treatment rooms offer such delights as an energising Laguna Spice Cocktail for face and body, and sensuous baths filled with milk and roses. While you are being pampered, listen out for Elton John, who keeps a *pied-à-l'eau* next door. *Fondamenta delle Zitelle 33, T 041 520 7022, www.palladiohotelspa.it*

Lido beaches

Catch a ferry from Isola del Tronchetto
(near the station) to Lido island, which is
surrounded by 12km of beaches. Though
many of the public ones (*spiaggia libera*)
leave a lot to be desired, you can have a
taste of belle époque glamour in the bars
and private beach clubs of Lido's stylish
hotels: the glorious art deco Des Bains
(T 041 526 5921) or the early 20th-century
Moorish-influenced Westin Excelsior (see
p096), with its luxurious bamboo beach
huts. Though the ethereal atmosphere
of Luchino Visconti's *Death in Venice* is
in very short supply in third-millennium
Lido and the aroma of exhaust fumes
shocks after the car-free bliss of Venice,
a hedonistic, pampered, sun-filled
experience can still be had (at a cost).
Especially during the film festival, which
runs for two weeks in early September.

Bucintoro Rowing Club

Many of the local *cantieri* (boatyards) host rowing clubs partly funded by the city council in order to preserve Venetian traditions. These offer lessons, sponsor regattas and hold social events. Founded in 1882, the Bucintoro Rowing Club is the oldest in Venice. It offers rowing (both seated, known as *voga all'inglese*, and in the unique Venetian style – standing up and facing forwards – called *voga alla veneta*), sailing and canoeing lessons and boat hire. Its Regata delle Befane (6th January) sees senior (55+) male members race from San Tomà to Rialto dressed as *La Befana*, a witch-type figure who, according to tradition, brings gifts to children who have been good over the previous year and coal (lumps of black sugar) to the naughty. *15 Punta della Dogana, T 041 520 5630, www.bucintoro.org*

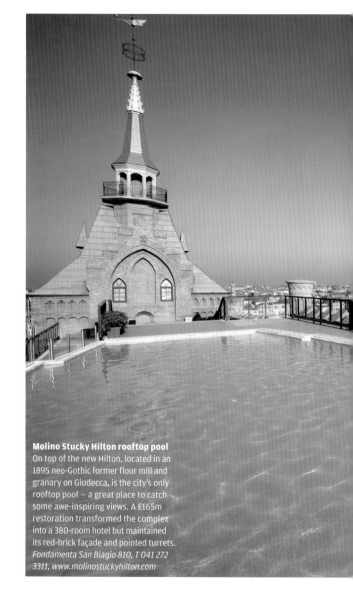

Molino Stucky Hilton rooftop pool
On top of the new Hilton, located in an
1895 neo-Gothic former flour mill and
granary on Giudecca, is the city's only
rooftop pool – a great place to catch
some awe-inspiring views. A £165m
restoration transformed the complex
into a 380-room hotel but maintained
its red-brick façade and pointed turrets.
*Fondamenta San Biagio 810, T 041 272
3311, www.molinostuckyhilton.com*

ESCAPES

WHERE TO GO IF YOU WANT TO LEAVE TOWN

Venice may be the highlight of any trip to the Veneto, but it is also a claustrophobic city where getting around is a slow, arduous process. When you need a day off from the crowds, you can choose from an array of picturesque places, many only an hour away.

Treviso – famous as the airport for cheap flights to Venice – is a pretty old town with great dining options, masses of hip designer clothing stores and a series of culinary festivals, including one dedicated to the Radicchio Trevigiano, a tasty chicory grown locally. Asolo is a small medieval walled town with breathtaking views and one of Italy's finest hotels, Villa Cipriani (Via Canova 298, T 042 352 3411), located in a villa formerly owned by Robert Browning, and Padua is a university town with lots to do and see. Vicenza was the home of 16th-century starchitect Andrea Palladio, who enriched his town with notable buildings such as the Teatro Olimpico and the Villa Rotonda, while Verona offers a compact concentration of history and culture, and a massive Roman arena in which to catch an enthralling outdoor opera performance.

But if it's beach respite you are after, head to Lido island (see p090). To recreate Thomas Mann's heady *Death in Venice*, it's best to avoid the ungroomed public beaches and splash out on a cabin for the day through one of the grand hotels, such as the Westin Excelsior (Lungomare Guglielmo Marconi 41, T 041 526 0201). *For full addresses, see Resources.*

Museo Gipsoteca Canova, Possagno

The small town of Possagno, situated amid the Asolan hills, features one of the most bizarre sights of the region – a huge 18th-century neoclassical temple. Designed by Antonio Canova, considered to be the last great Italian sculptor, it rises above the houses and offers amazing views. Canova's family home, and two annexes built in the 1830s and 1957 respectively (the latter by Venetian architect Carlo Scarpa), now house a comprehensive and memorable collection of his work, including some of his lesser-known paintings and plaster models. The Museo Gipsoteca Canova is one of the most appealing small museums in Europe, and the Scarpa wing shows the architect's skill in creating unexpected drama in a constrained space. *Piazza Canova 84, T 042 354 4323, www.museocanova.it*

Bassano del Grappa

The historic centre of Bassano del Grappa is alluringly photogenic and only just over an hour by train from Venice. It has narrow cobbled streets and colonnaded squares, it sits at the foot of Monte Grappa with the snow-crested Dolomites in the background and it has a river – the Brenta – gushing through it. Its main landmark is a long wooden bridge (above), designed in 1569 by Andrea Palladio,

which, during prime *aperitivo* time, holds the overflow for happy drinkers spilling out of a small *grapperia* called Nardini (T 042 422 7741). Grappa sometimes gets a bad rap as a rustic, unrefined drink; however, the newer grappas are smoother and more polished, and pack a pleasing punch. The story of the spirit is explained at the Museo della Grappa (T 042 452 4426), not far from Palladio's bridge.

Torcello

Venice's original settlement is a charming excursion from the city (take the Linea 12 ferry from the Fondamenta Nuove stop). This sleepy island used to be a bustling town with 20,000 inhabitants; today the main piazza is overgrown with weeds, with two churches in splendid isolation. The Basilica di Santa Maria Assunta (above) is the oldest building in Venice lagoon, founded in the 7th century, although most of it is an 11th-century reconstruction. On the walls and apse are some fantastic mosaics (left): a charming Madonna and Child on a gold background, and a chilling Last Judgement with hellish details, such as serpents crawling through skulls. The Church of Santa Fosca, also dating to the 11th century, is built to a Greek-cross plan. Remember to check the time of the return boat, or you may be in for a long wait.

Riviera del Brenta

The section of the river Brenta between Padua and Venice became a favourite building site for the Venetian aristocracy in the 16th century. These villas were mostly summer residences where the gentry would while away the months between June and November. There are about 100 still left standing today; some inhabited, others abandoned. Among the most interesting are Villa Fóscari (T 041 547 0012), designed by Andrea Palladio; Villa Widmann Rezzonico Fóscari (T 041 424 973), for its delightful garden; the ruins of Villa Barchessa Valmarana (T 041 426 6387) – the family who owned the villa destroyed it in the 19th century to avoid paying luxury taxes; and Villa Pisani (above; T 049 502 270), for its sheer opulent overkill and its huge ballroom fresco by Tiepolo.

NOTES

SKETCHES AND MEMOS

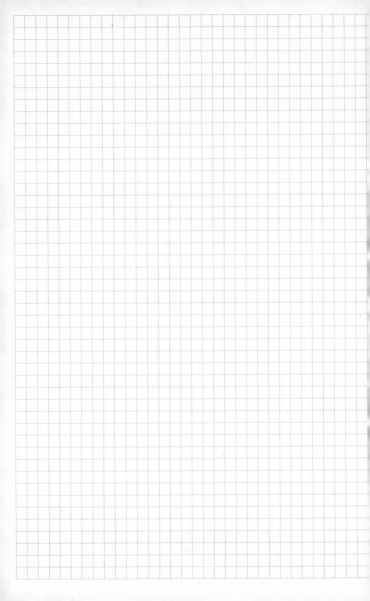

RESOURCES

CITY GUIDE DIRECTORY

HOTELS

ADDRESSES AND ROOM RATES

Avogaria 016
 Room rates:
 price on request
 Calle dell'Avogaria 1629
 T 041 296 0491
 www.avogaria.com

Des Bains 090
 Room rates:
 double, from €125
 Lungomare Marconi 17
 Lido
 T 041 526 5921

Casa de Uscoli 022
 Room rates:
 double, from €210;
 Suite dell'Alcova, €350;
 Suite della Salute, from €450
 Campo Santo Stefano 2818
 T 041 241 0669
 www.casadeuscoli.com

Charming House DD694 030
 Room rates:
 double, from €280;
 Luxury Suite, from €470
 Ramo San Cristoforo 694
 T 041 277 0262
 www.dd724.it

Charming House DD724 030
 Room rates:
 double, from €280;
 Superior Room, from €370
 Ramo da Mula 724
 T 041 277 0262
 www.dd724.it

Charming House IQs 030
 Room rates:
 double, from €280
 Campiello Querini Stampalia 4425
 T 041 241 0062
 www.dd724.it

Hotel Cipriani 016
 Room rates:
 double, from €870;
 Palladio Suite, from €6,800
 Fondamenta San Giovanni 10
 T 041 520 7744
 www.hotelcipriani.com

Villa Cipriani 096
 Room rates:
 double, from €165
 Via Canova 298
 Asolo
 T 042 352 3411

Ca' Gottardi 018
 Room rates:
 double, from €130;
 Suite 28, from €180;
 Room 36, from €180
 Strada Nuova 2283
 T 041 275 9333
 www.cagottardi.com

Ca Maria Adele 017
 Room rates:
 Deluxe, from €330;
 La Sala Noir, from €440;
 Suite 339, from €495
 Rio Terà dei Catecumeni 111
 T 041 520 3078
 www.camariaadele.it

Hotel Metropole 024
 Room rates:
 double, from €210;
 Room 405, €600;
 Damasco Suite, €1,600
 Riva degli Schiavoni 4149
 T 041 520 5044
 www.hotelmetropole.com

Molino Stucky Hilton 016
Room rates:
double, from €275
Fondamenta San Biagio 810
T 041 272 3311
www.molinostuckyhilton.com
Ca' Nigra Lagoon Resort 028
Room rates:
double, from €150;
Room 11, from €170
Campo San Simeon Grande 927
T 041 275 0047
www.hotelcanigra.com
Novecento Boutique Hotel 016
Room rates:
double, from €140
Calle del Dose 2683
T 041 241 3765
www.novecento.biz
Palazzina Grassi 016
Room rates:
double, from €190
Calle Grassi 3247
T 041 528 4644
www.palazzinagrassi.it
**Palazzo Barbarigo sul Canal
Grande** 016
Room rates:
double, from €180
Calle Corner 2765
T 041 740 172
www.hotelphilosophy.net
Ca' Pisani 026
Room rates:
double, from €210;
Junior Suite, from €370
Rio Terà António Foscarini 979a
T 041 240 1411
www.capisanihotel.it

Ca' Sagredo 019
Room rates:
double, from €300;
Room 103, from €1,100;
Grand Canal Suite Prestige, from €1,100
Campo Santa Sofia 4198
T 041 241 3111
www.casagredohotel.com
Hotel Saturnia 026
Room rates:
double, €490
Calle Larga XXII Marzo 2398
T 041 520 8377
Westin Excelsior 096
Room rates:
double, from €330
Lungomare Guglielmo Marconi 41
Lido
T 041 526 0201
www.starwoodhotels.com

WALLPAPER* CITY GUIDES

Editorial Director
Richard Cook

Art Director
Loran Stosskopf
City Editor
Giovanna Dunmall
Editor
Rachael Moloney
Executive
Managing Editor
Jessica Firmin
Travel Bookings Editor
Sara Henrichs

Chief Designer
Daniel Shrimpton
Designer
Lara Collins
Map Illustrator
Russell Bell

Photography Editor
Christopher Lands
Photography Assistant
Robin Key

Chief Sub-Editor
Jeremy Case
Sub-Editors
Vicky McGinlay
Stephen Patience
Melanie Wells
Editorial Assistant
Ella Marshall

Intern
Rosa Bertoli

Wallpaper* Group
Editor-in-Chief
Tony Chambers
Publisher
Neil Sumner

Contributors
Gloria Beggiato
Alessio and Nicola Campa
Meirion Pritchard
Francesco Pugliese
Ellie Stathaki

Wallpaper* ® is a
registered trademark
of IPC Media Limited

All prices are correct at
time of going to press,
but are subject to change.

PHAIDON

Phaidon Press Limited
Regent's Wharf
All Saints Street
London N1 9PA

Phaidon Press Inc
180 Varick Street
New York, NY 10014

Phaidon® is a registered
trademark of Phaidon
Press Limited

www.phaidon.com

First published 2008
© 2008 IPC Media Limited

ISBN 978 0 7148 4753 5

A CIP Catalogue record for
this book is available from
the British Library.

All rights reserved.
No part of this publication
may be reproduced, stored
in a retrieval system or
transmitted, in any form
or by any means,
electronic, mechanical,
photocopying, recording
or otherwise, without
the prior permission of
Phaidon Press.

Printed in China

PHOTOGRAPHERS

**Bildarchiv Monheim/
Artur**
Fondaco dei Turchi,
pp010-011

**Bildarchiv Monheim
GmbH/Alamy**
Brenta Riviera, pp102-103

Bridgemanart.com
Torcello, p100

Michael Kneffel/Artur
Ca' d'Oro, p013

Massimo Listri/Corbis
Museo Gipsoteca Canova,
Possagno, p097

Florian Monheim/Artur
Rialto bridge, pp034-035

Sarah Quill/Alamy
Torre dell'Orologio, p012

Francesco Radino
Ex-Saffa housing
development, pp068-069

Daniele Resini
Arsenale, pp014-015
Ca Maria Adele, p017
Ca' Gottardi, p018
Ca' Sagredo, p019,
pp020-021
Casa de Uscoli, p022

Hotel Metropole,
pp024-025
Ca' Pisani, p026, p027
Ca' Nigra Lagoon Resort,
pp028-029
Charming House DD724,
pp030-031
Torrefazione Marchi, p033
Riviera, p038
Harry's Bar, p039
Il Ridotto, p041
Osteria San Marco,
pp042-043
Vecio Fritolin, p044
Skyline Bar, p045
Lineadombra, pp046-047
Naranzaria, pp048-049
Andrea Zanin, pp050-051
Restaurant De Pisis and
B-Bar, pp052-053
Osteria Santa
Marina, p054
Aurora, p055
Centrale Restaurant
Lounge, pp056-057
Dogado Lounge,
pp060-061
Isotta Dardilli, p063
Casa Gardella alle
Zattere, p065
Stazione Ferroviaria
Santa Lucia, pp066-067
Santa Maria Gloriosa dei
Frari, pp070-071
Angela Greco, pp074-075
Antonia Miletto, p076
Massimo Micheluzzi, p077
VizioVirtù, pp078-079

Le Forcole di Saverio Pastor,
pp080-081
Marina e Susanna Sent, p082
Trois, p083
Attombri, pp084-085
Studio Mirabilia, pp086-087
Lido beaches, pp090-091
Bucintoro Rowing Club,
pp092-093
Molino Stucky Hilton rooftop
pool, pp094-095
Bassano del Grappa,
pp098-099

**Worldwide Picture
Library/Alamy**
Torcello, p101

VENICE

A COLOUR-CODED GUIDE TO THE HOT 'HOODS

CANNAREGIO

Venice's main entry point, and a tranquil alternative to the more well-trodden *sestieri*

LA GIUDECCA

A historically run-down archipelago that is now attracting some serious investment

SANTA CROCE AND SAN POLO

With hip bars, restaurants and the Rialto markets, this central district is always bustling

CASTELLO

The Arsenale is where the big guns of art and architecture gather for the Venice Biennales

DORSODURO

Head here to find world-renowned galleries and some of the city's most desirable hotels

SAN MARCO

La Serenissima at its most iconic – time-worn stones, flocks of tourists and the Campanile

For a full description of each neighbourhood, see the Introduction.
Featured venues are colour-coded, according to the district in which they are located.